Holistic Love Making

Dr. Nigel Harrison DD ND

authorHOUSE®

AuthorHouse™
1663 Liberty Drive
Bloomington, IN 47403
www.authorhouse.com
Phone: 1-800-839-8640

First published by AuthorHouse 7/9/2010

ISBN: 978-1-4520-3538-3 (e)
ISBN: 978-1-4520-3539-0 (sc)

Library of Congress Control Number: 2010908637

Printed in the United States of America
Bloomington, Indiana

This book is printed on acid-free paper.

Contents

Holistic

Love

Making

Making Love
Mind Body And Spirit

MASSAGE HER TOP TO BOTTOM
SERVE HER FRESH JUICE AND FRUITS

READ HER POETRY, DANCE TOGETHER,
FREE PLAY AND HAVE FUN

HAVE A SPECIAL DAY OF THE WEEK
JUST FOR HER
FRIDAY, SATURDAY OR SUNDAY

IF you love it enough, anything will talk with you. "George Washington Carver"

The Rules

NO NEGATIVE THINKING

NO NEGATIVE EMOTION

NO CRITICISM

NO COMPLAINT

NO SADNESS

NO DOUBT

NO FEAR

NO HITTING

NO INSULTING

NO CURSING

Man love because he is love. He seeks joy, for he is joy. He thirsts for god, for he is composed of god and he cannot exist with out him. "Sathya Sai Baba"

Rules

WOMAN THE GIFT AND MAN THE STRENGTH

FIND EACH OTHER GIFTS

FIND EACH OTHER STRENGTH

KNOW EACH OTHERS WORTH

    SIMPLE

LOVE AND RESPECT

LOVING WORDS AND LOVING TOUCH

KNOW BOTH ARE SACRED

VERY SPECIAL!!!

WE ARE CHOOSEN

WE ARE SPECIAL TOGETHER

I bless the person of conditions as channel of my prosperity, but god is the source of my supply "Catherine Ponder"

Dressing

COTTON CLOTHING

VERY COMFORTABLE

 LOOSE OUTFIT

OR

HALF NUDE

WHAT WORKS FOR YOU

Sacret Place

CREATE A SPECIAL

PLACE FOR LOVE IN YOUR HOME

WITH FLOWERS, STONES AND WATER

WORDS OF APPRECIATION AND MUSIC

As human beings, our greatness lies not so much in being able to remake the world as in being able to remake ourselves "Mahatma Gandhi"

Ritual Of Love

RITUAL OF APPRECIATION

RITUAL OF THANK YOU

RITUAL I WANT YOU

RITUAL YOU ARE MY QUEEN

RITUAL YOU ARE SWEET AND SEXY

RITUAL YOU ARE PURE

RITUAL OF WHOLE AND COMPLETE

Do not be afraid stand still, and see the salvation of the lord "Exodus 14:13"

Forms

HOLISTIC LOVE MAKING

AS THEY ARE 3-7 LEVELS

LEVELS	FORM/POSITION
1. MISSIONARY LOTUS POSITION	
2. STAR AND WIND AND DOUBLE STAR	CARESSING AND KISSING
3. ICE-CREAM AND CONE	
4. SCISSORS AND CUT	

To love one self is the beginning of a life long romance "Oscar Wilde"

Etiquette

PAMPER HER

SERVE HER

MASSAGE HER

RUN HER BATH

SPEAK WORD OF KINDNESS TO HER

ENCOURAGE HER

KNOW HER GIFTS AND STRENGTH

SPEAK SOFT, DISCUSS THINGS IN A
RESPECTFUL AND CALM STATE OF MIND

<u>SECRET</u>:   THE MORE YOU GIVE TO HER THE
MORE SHE WILL GIVE TO YOU.
THAT'S HER NATURE

DO IT TO EACH OTHER

The greatest fear of all for a human being is to be unloved and alone "Greg Baer"

Affirmations

WRITE DOWN FIVE THINGS YOU ADMIRE
ABOUT HER
THEN WRITE TEN THINGS
TILL YOU CAN WRITE FIFTH THINGS YOU CAN
ADMIRE AND CAN APPRECIATE ABOUT HER

<u>EXAMPLE:</u>

I ADMIRE AND APPRECIATE YOUR KINDNESS

I ADMIRE AND APPRECIATE YOUR SUPPORT

I ADMIRE AND APPRECIATE YOUR SMARTS

I ADMIRE AND APPRECIATE YOUR GIFT OF
KEEPING THE FAMILY TOGETHER AND PEACE
AMONG THE CHILDREN

I ADMIRE AND APPRECIATE YOU FOR ALWAYS
BEING
THERE FOR ME

I THANK YOU FOR BEING YOU

YOU ARE BEAUTIFUL AND SPECIAL

I VALUE YOUR GIFTS AND STRENGTH

God Is Love "John 4:16"

Positions

USING THE DOMINANT HAND
THAT YOU WRITE WITH
TOUCH HER HEART CENTER

AND

HER TOUCHING YOUR
HEART CENTER

LOOK IN EACH OTHER EYES
AND DO THE AFFIRMATIONS
SEE IN EACH OTHER BEAUTY AND
DECLARE IT
SEE THE LOVE THE JOY AND FEEL IT
FILL EACH OTHER NEEDS AND WANT

Thou art ever with me, and all that I have is thine. "Luke 15:31"

To Enhance

ANY SACRED LOVE STYLE
LIKE KARMA SUTRA AND
TANTRA

STYLE THAT DEAL WITH
BREATHING AND FORMS - TO
DEEPEN AND INTENSIFY THE
EXOTIC BOND

AFFIRMATION, PURE HEART, RELAXATION
AND MAKE IT FUN AND FEEL THE
POSITIVE ENERGY WILL TAKE
YOU MUCH FURTHER

Make you work to be keeping with your purpose.
"Leonardo Da Vinci"

Mind Set

PEACEFUL

RELAXING

FUN LOVING WITH
SOFT SLOW KISSING

AND

GENTLE CARESSING

SOFT TONE VOICE OF
LOVE AND APPRECIATION

Truth knows no opposites the science of the mine. "Science Of The Mind" Page 189

Sacred Space

PICK SOFT COLORS

LIGHT -   GREEN

LIGHT -   BLUE

LIGHT -   RED

VIOLET -   PURPLE

SOFT COLOR FREQUENCY ENHANCE
HUMAN VIBRATION

SACRED SPACE CAN BE IN THE
LIVINGROOM, OR WHERE YOU
ARE COMFORTABLE IN THE
HOUSE WITH YOUR PARTNER

Deserve your dreams. " Octavio Paz"

Intuitive Love Making

INTUITIVE LOVE MAKING IS
ALSO SIMPLE
EYES CLOSED OR COVERED

TAKE A COUPLE DEEP BREATH
RELAX BE AWARE OF YOUR
GUT FEELING OR
DANTIEN - BELOW THE NAVEL AREA
LISTEN TO YOUR PARTNER
BREATHING

LISTEN TO YOUR OWN BREATHING
ASK YOURSELF WHERE DOES
MY MATE NEED TO BE TOUCHED
TO EXPERIENCE LOVE AND
RELEASE NEGATIVE EMOTION

LISTEN AND REACT FROM INSIDE
OUT

God is out refuge and strength, a very present help in time of trouble. "Psalms 46:1"

Intuitive Love Making

BE AWARE OF THE CHAKRAS

PUT YOUR HANDS ABOVE
THE CHAKRA AREAS

AND FEEL THE POSITIVE
ENERGY

AND

SEND YOUR MATE
LOVE AND IT WILL
BE RETURNED TO YOU
100 FOLD BACK

INTUITIVE KISSING

INTUITIVE TOUCHING

INTUITIVE WORDS

Peace cannot be kept by force it can only be achieved by understanding. "Albert Einstein"

A Woman Needs

1.   A WOMAN NEED -   <u>EMOTIONAL</u>,
     <u>PSYCHOLOGICAL</u>, <u>MENTAL</u> SECURITY

2.   A WOMAN NEED -   <u>HEALTHY ATTENTION</u>
     EG: FEEL UNDERSTOOD AND BEING
     LISTENING TO

3.   A WOMAN NEED -   <u>GOOD LOVING</u>
     EG: PASSION, LOVE, RESPECT

ABOVE ALL A VISION FOR THE RELATIONSHIP

Prayer in action is love, and love in action is service. "Mother Teresa A Simple Path"

A Man Need

THREE THINGS

<u>SPIRIT</u>

1. A MAN NEEDS TO BE VALUED
    APPRECIATED FOR HIS
    PRINCIPLE, CHARACTER,
    VISION

<u>MIND</u>

2. A MAN NEEDS MIND, LOVE,
    RESPECT

<u>SPIRIT</u>

3. A MAN NEEDS HEALTHY FORM
    AND HEALTHY RELEASE
                  OF
    TOXIC EMOTION AND STRESS
    AND A VISION FOR HIMSELF

Love one another and you will be happy its as simple and as difficult as that. "Micheal Leunig"

LOVING BONDING

STRONG RELATIONSHIP

FUN LOVING

RESPECT AND VALUE

MAN KNOW YOUR WOMAN WORTH

WOMANKNOW YOUR MAN WORTH

The future is made of the same stuff as the present. "Simone Well"

Body Hygiene

A MAN SHOULD SHOWER TWICE A DAY
MORNING AND EVENING AND USING
COLOGNE OR OIL HIS FAVORITE SMELL

ALSO DETOX PANCREAS, COLON, KIDNEY,
LIVER, BLOOD CLEANSING
A MAN SHOULD EXERCISE, NO GYM
MEMBERSHIP

DO PUSH UP 100-500 A DAY
PUSH UP GIVE YOU STAMINA AND
ENDURANCE
IN THE BEDROOM

A MAN SHOULD SHAVE UNDERARM AND
CROCH AREA ONCE A MONTH USE
A STEAMROOM AND TAKE A BATH
FOR 20 MIN

IN THE SUMMER EAT A LOT OF FRUITS AND
VEGETABLE

IN THE WINTER EAT SALMON, TURKEY
AND CHICKEN

NO SUGAR, NO ALCOHOL, NO CAFFEINE

Never let what you fear intrude on what you know. "Sun Rain"

Hygiene For Woman

A WOMAN SHOULD SHOWER TWICE A DAY
MORNING AND EVENING AND USE PERFUME
OR OIL HER FAVORITE SMELL ALSO,
DOUCHE WITH VINEGAR
ALSO DETOX PANCREAS, COLON, KIDNEY
LIVER, BLOOD CLEANSING

WOMAN SHOULD EXERCISE, NO GYM
MEMBERSHIP
SHE SHOULD DO SPEED WALKING,
POWER WALK, CARDIO WITH
FREE WEIGHT 5 - 10 LB

WOMAN SHOULD SHAVE PRIVATE AREA

WOMAN SHOULD TAKE A BATH WITH
BAKING SODA, SEASALT, 3% HYDRO
PEROXIDE

IN SUMMER EAT A LOT OF FRUITS AND
VEGETABLE

IN WINTER SALMON, CHICKEN, TURKEY

NO SUGAR, CAFFEINE, NO ALCOHOL

AND 5 - 10 MIN MEDITATION TO DISCOVER
PERSONAL POWER

Loneliness can be conquered only by those who can bear solitude. "Paul Tillich"

Desire A Baby

WHEN IT COMES TO CHILDREN SOME
INDIVIDUAL HAVE PREFERENCE
TO BOY OR GIRL

I CAN TELL YOU TO ASK FOR A
HEALTHY, HAPPY

      AND

A CHILD OF DIVINE WISDOM,
WHO HAS A MIND AND
HEART THAT IS GOOD

HONORABLE, VIRTUES, SMART, AND
WILL MAKE A DIFFERENCE IN THE
WORLD FOR GOOD

A GIFT FROM GOD

BEFORE MAKING LOVE THE COUPLE
SHOULD PRAY TOGETHER AND MAKE
THERE REQUEST TO GOD BE KNOWN
AND ALSO THAT THERE UNION TOGETHER
BE BLESSED WITH LOVE, JOY, HAPPINESS

*Nowhere can man fine a quieter or more untroubled retreat than in his own soul.
"Marcus Aurelius"*

What To Have

HAVE   -   LAUGHTER

HAVE   -   FUN

HAVE   -   HAPPINESS

HAVE   -   JOY

HAVE   -   PEACE

HAVE   -   HEALTHY LOVE MAKING

GROW WITH IT TOGETHER
ANY LOVE MAKING WITH <u>SADNESS</u>,
<u>DOUBT</u>, <u>FEAR, ANGER</u> IS NEGATIVE
AND ABUSIVE LOVING AND TOUCHING

BE POSITIVE AND THE RELATIONSHIP
WILL BE STRONG

BE NEGATIVE AND THE RELATIONSHIP
BECOMES WEAK AND DIE

Looking within, finding stillness free from fear, free from attachment, knowing the sweet joy of the way. "The Dhammapada"

Unconditional

YOU MUST HAVE UNCONDITIONAL
LOVE FOR YOURSELF
AND FOR YOUR MATE

LOVE IS THE HIGHEST VIBRATION

YOU LOVE YOURSELF

YOU RESPECT YOURSELF

YOU RESPECT YOURSELF

YOU PROTECT YOURSELF

SEE THE WORLD THROUGH THE
EYES OF LOVE

AND LIVE FROM THE HEART
OF LOVE

www.ingramcontent.com/pod-product-compliance
Lightning Source LLC
Chambersburg PA
CBHW050338290526
45785CB00006B/2551